ANGORA RABBIT

The ultimate guide to caring for, grooming, and enjoying your fluffy fiber friend

ANTHONY E. WINDLEY

Table of Contents

CHAPTER ONE
INTRODUCTION TO ANGORA RABBITS

Angora rabbits are one of the oldest domesticated rabbit breeds, celebrated for their luxurious wool and gentle demeanor. Originating centuries ago, these rabbits have been bred for their high-quality fiber, which is prized for its softness, warmth, and lightweight texture. With their long, silky coats and calm temperament, Angora rabbits have become popular not only as fiber-producing animals but also as charming companions. Their unique needs and captivating presence make them a fascinating addition to the world of small pets and livestock. Understanding their history, the variety of breeds, and what makes them so special is essential for anyone considering raising or caring for these remarkable animals.

The History and Origins of Angora Rabbits

The origins of Angora rabbits can be traced back to Ankara, Turkey (historically known as Angora), where they were first bred for their wool. This region was also home to other luxurious fiber-producing animals, such as the Angora goat and Angora cat. By the 18th century, Angora rabbits had made their way to Europe, becoming particularly popular in France, where they were kept by nobility as exotic pets. Over time, their reputation spread globally, and they became a cornerstone of the fiber industry due to their ability to produce soft, warm, and hypoallergenic wool. Today, Angora rabbits are bred worldwide, not only for their fiber but also as show animals and pets. Their rich history reflects the human appreciation for their extraordinary wool and gentle, sociable nature.

Overview of Angora Rabbit Breeds

Angora rabbits are not a single breed but a category encompassing several distinct breeds, each with unique characteristics and wool types. The most well-known breeds include the English Angora, French Angora, German Angora, Giant Angora, and Satin Angora. The English Angora is perhaps the most recognizable, with its fluffy appearance and wool even covering its face and ears. French Angoras have a sleeker appearance, with wool concentrated on their bodies rather than their extremities. German Angoras are highly valued in commercial fiber production due to their consistent wool yield. The Giant Angora, a larger breed, is also a significant wool producer, while the Satin Angora is known for its lustrous and shiny coat. Each breed offers unique opportunities and challenges for owners, whether they are kept for fiber, companionship, or exhibition. Understanding these differences is essential for selecting the right breed for your needs and lifestyle.

Why Angora Rabbits Are Unique and Special

Angora rabbits are unlike any other rabbit breed, thanks to their remarkable ability to produce luxurious wool that rivals some of the finest textiles in the world. Their wool, known as Angora fiber, is renowned for its exceptional softness, warmth, and lightweight properties, making it a prized material in high-quality garments and accessories. Beyond their fiber production, Angora rabbits are also known for their gentle, friendly nature, making them ideal pets for those willing to meet their specific care requirements. However, their uniqueness comes with responsibility; Angora rabbits require regular grooming to prevent their thick coats from matting, as well as a diet rich in fiber to support their overall health. Their calm demeanor, combined with their stunning appearance and practical contributions to fiber arts, makes them a truly special addition to any household or farm. Raising Angora rabbits can be a deeply rewarding experience, blending creativity, companionship, and sustainability in a way few other animals can.

CHAPTER TWO

UNDERSTANDING ANGORA RABBIT BEHAVIOR AND TRAITS

Angora rabbits are among the most enchanting breeds in the world, admired for their luxurious fur and unique personality traits. Understanding their behavior and characteristics is crucial for ensuring their well-being and fostering a strong bond between pet and owner. Below, we explore their physical attributes, personality traits, and daily habits in depth.

Physical Characteristics: Fur, Size, and Features

Angora rabbits are best known for their strikingly soft and dense wool, which sets them apart from other rabbit breeds. Their fur is not just a defining feature but also requires meticulous care.

- **Fur**: Angora wool grows continuously, resembling that of cashmere or mohair. Depending on the specific variety—English, French, Giant, or Satin Angora—the texture, density, and grooming needs of their coats vary. This luxurious fur is highly prized in the textile industry and must be combed regularly to prevent matting and reduce the risk of wool block, a condition caused by ingesting too much fur.

- **Size and Build**: Angora rabbits typically weigh between 5 and 12 pounds, with variations depending on the specific breed. They have a compact body structure, with French and Giant Angoras being the largest, while English Angoras are comparatively smaller. Their rounded head and tufted ears, often adorned with soft fur, give them a distinctive appearance.

- **Distinctive Features**: Apart from their fur, Angora rabbits are noted for their gentle eyes and expressive faces, which can be incredibly communicative. Their strong, muscular hind legs enable them to hop gracefully, and their sensitive whiskers help them navigate their environment.

Personality and Social Behavior

Angora rabbits are gentle, intelligent, and social animals. Their unique personalities make them delightful companions, but they require understanding and patience to thrive.

- **Temperament**: Angoras are typically calm and docile, making them ideal for households that value a quieter pet. They enjoy human interaction and can form strong bonds with their owners when given consistent attention.

- **Social Nature**: While Angora rabbits can adapt well to living alone, they are inherently social creatures that enjoy the company of other rabbits. If kept in pairs or groups, they exhibit playful and cooperative behavior, such as grooming each other or engaging in lighthearted chases.

- **Emotional Sensitivity**: Angoras are sensitive to changes in their environment. Sudden noises, unfamiliar scents, or new surroundings can cause stress, which may manifest in behaviors such as hiding or reduced appetite. Building trust and maintaining a stable environment is crucial for their emotional well-being.

- **Training and Intelligence**: These rabbits are surprisingly intelligent and can be trained to use a litter box or even respond to simple commands. Positive reinforcement, such as treats and gentle encouragement, works best to motivate them.

Daily Activity Patterns and Communication

Understanding the daily routines and communication methods of Angora rabbits can enhance your ability to cater to their needs and interpret their behavior.

1. **Activity Levels**: Angora rabbits are crepuscular, meaning they are most active during the early morning and late evening hours. These times are ideal for play and interaction. During the day, they prefer resting in a quiet, shaded area, while nighttime is often spent in subdued activity.

2. **Play and Exercise**: Regular physical activity is essential for maintaining their health. Angoras

enjoy exploring their surroundings, chewing on safe toys, and engaging in digging behaviors. Providing them with ample space and rabbit-safe objects to interact with can prevent boredom and destructive habits.

3. **Communication**: Angoras use subtle body language and vocalizations to communicate. For example:

- **Binkying**: This joyous leap into the air signifies happiness and excitement.
- **Thumping**: A loud thump of the hind legs can indicate fear or frustration.
- **Nudging**: A gentle nudge with the nose is often a sign of curiosity or a request for attention.
- **Purring**: A soft, grinding noise made with their teeth usually indicates contentment.

4. **Feeding and Grooming Patterns**: Angoras are grazers and enjoy small, frequent meals

throughout the day. Their diet should primarily consist of high-quality hay, supplemented with fresh vegetables and rabbit pellets. Grooming, as a natural behavior, helps them maintain their coats, but owners must assist with brushing to manage their dense fur.

Overall, Understanding the behavior and traits of Angora rabbits is essential for providing the best care and nurturing a strong bond. From their luxurious fur and unique personalities to their communicative behaviors and daily habits, Angoras are remarkable pets. With proper attention, patience, and love, these gentle creatures can thrive and bring immense joy to their owners.

CHAPTER THREE

PREPARING FOR AN ANGORA RABBIT

Welcoming an Angora rabbit into your home is a rewarding experience that requires thoughtful preparation. These charming and luxurious rabbits have specific needs, and getting started on the right foot will ensure their health and happiness. From choosing the right breed to setting up their environment, this guide offers a comprehensive approach to getting ready for your new Angora rabbit.

Choosing the Right Breed for Your Needs

Angora rabbits come in several distinct breeds, each with unique characteristics. Selecting the right one for your lifestyle and goals involves understanding their differences and assessing what aligns with your preferences.

- **English Angora**: Known for their compact size and extensive wool coverage, English Angoras are ideal for those who enjoy grooming and appreciate a truly luxurious coat. They are among the most wool-rich breeds, requiring daily care to prevent matting.

- **French Angora**: Slightly larger and less wool-covered on the face and ears, French Angoras are easier to maintain than their English counterparts. Their calm demeanor makes them a good choice for first-time Angora owners.

- **Giant Angora**: As the largest of the Angora breeds, Giant Angoras produce abundant wool and require ample space. They are a good fit for those interested in harvesting wool but are less ideal for smaller homes.

- **Satin Angora**: Renowned for their silky, shiny wool, Satin Angoras are smaller and produce less fiber than other breeds, but their fur is of exceptional quality. They are a great choice for fiber enthusiasts looking for premium material.

- **Consider Your Goals**: If you're interested in producing wool, select a breed known for high-quality fiber production, like the Giant or Satin Angora. For companionship, the temperament and grooming requirements of the English or French Angora may be more appealing.

Selecting a Healthy Rabbit: What to Look For

Choosing a healthy rabbit is crucial for ensuring your pet starts its life with you in the best condition possible. Whether you're purchasing from a breeder, adopting from a shelter, or buying from a pet store, take time to carefully assess the rabbit's health and environment.

- **Physical Examination**:

  - ✓ Look for bright, clear eyes without any signs of discharge.
  - ✓ Check the ears for cleanliness and absence of mites or redness.
  - ✓ The nose should be dry and free of mucus. A runny nose could indicate respiratory issues.
  - ✓ Inspect the rabbit's teeth for alignment and overgrowth. Malocclusion can lead to feeding difficulties.

- ✓ Feel for a smooth, healthy coat. Fur should be dense, soft, and free of bald spots or excessive shedding.
- ✓ Examine the feet for sores and check that the nails are not overgrown.

- **Behavior and Temperament**:

  - ✓ A healthy rabbit is alert, curious, and responsive to its surroundings.
  - ✓ Avoid rabbits that appear lethargic, excessively shy, or aggressive.

- **Environmental Conditions**:

  - ✓ Assess the cleanliness of the environment where the rabbit is being housed. Unsanitary conditions may lead to health problems.
  - ✓ Ask the breeder or seller about the rabbit's diet, vaccinations, and any history of illness.

Initial Supplies and Home Setup

Creating a safe and comfortable environment for your Angora rabbit is essential for their well-being. Their unique needs call for specialized supplies and thoughtful planning.

- **Housing**:

  - ✓ Choose a spacious cage or hutch with enough room for the rabbit to hop, stretch, and move freely. The enclosure should be at least four times the size of your rabbit when fully stretched out.
  - ✓ Provide solid flooring with a section of soft bedding to prevent sores on their sensitive feet. Avoid wire flooring, which can cause discomfort and injuries.
  - ✓ Ensure the enclosure is well-ventilated, secure, and located in a quiet, temperature-controlled area. Angora rabbits are sensitive to extreme heat or cold.

- **Litter Box**:

  ✓ Rabbits can be litter trained, so place a litter box with rabbit-safe litter in their enclosure. Avoid clumping or scented litters, as these can harm your pet.

- **Grooming Supplies**:

  ✓ A high-quality grooming brush and comb are essential for maintaining their dense fur.

  ✓ Scissors or clippers designed for pet grooming will help you trim matted fur and wool.

  ✓ Purchase a nail trimmer suitable for small animals to keep their nails in check.

- **Feeding Supplies**:

  ✓ Provide a sturdy, tip-proof food bowl and a water bottle or heavy water dish.

  ✓ Stock up on high-quality hay, which should form the majority of their diet, as well as rabbit pellets and fresh vegetables.

✓ Avoid sugary treats or foods high in carbohydrates, as these can upset their digestive system.

- **Enrichment Items**:

  ✓ Angora rabbits thrive with mental and physical stimulation. Offer toys, such as wooden chews, cardboard tubes, and tunnels, to keep them engaged.

  ✓ Provide space for supervised exercise outside the cage. A rabbit-proofed room or enclosed playpen works well for this purpose.

- **Safety Considerations**:

  ✓ Rabbit-proof your home by covering electrical cords and removing any toxic plants or chemicals from areas your rabbit will explore.

✓ Ensure their enclosure and play areas are free from predators, sharp objects, or potential hazards.

Proper preparation is the foundation for a fulfilling relationship with your Angora rabbit. By choosing the right breed, ensuring you select a healthy pet, and creating a safe and comfortable home, you set the stage for a happy and rewarding experience. Angora rabbits are special companions that thrive with attentive care, and with the right preparations, they can bring years of joy to your life.

CHAPTER FOUR
CREATING THE IDEAL HABITAT

Providing your rabbit with a well-designed habitat is essential for its physical and emotional well-being. Rabbits are sensitive creatures that require a secure, comfortable, and stimulating environment to thrive. Whether you're considering indoor or outdoor housing, it's important to address all aspects of their living conditions to ensure they remain happy and healthy. This guide explores housing options, the setup process, and strategies to maintain a safe and inviting habitat for your rabbit.

Indoor vs. Outdoor Housing Options

Choosing between indoor and outdoor housing for your rabbit depends on several factors, including your living arrangements, climate, and personal preferences. Both options have advantages and challenges, so understanding the specifics is key to making an informed decision.

- **Indoor Housing**:

Keeping your rabbit indoors offers better protection from predators, harsh weather conditions, and temperature extremes. Indoor environments also allow for more frequent interaction between you and your pet.

Advantages:

- Climate control ensures your rabbit is not exposed to excessive heat, cold, or humidity.
- Greater opportunity for bonding, as indoor rabbits are more integrated into daily life.
- Reduced risk of attacks from predators, including dogs, cats, and wild animals.

Challenges:

- Rabbits need adequate space, which can be challenging in smaller homes.
- Home environments must be rabbit-proofed to prevent chewing on furniture, wires, or harmful objects.

- **Outdoor Housing**:

Outdoor housing allows rabbits to enjoy a more natural environment with fresh air and opportunities for exercise. However, it requires careful planning to ensure their safety.

Advantages:

- Outdoor setups can be larger, providing ample space for exercise and exploration.
- Exposure to natural light and fresh air supports overall health.

Challenges:

- Predators and environmental hazards pose significant risks.

- Weather conditions, including extreme heat or cold, can be dangerous without proper insulation and shelter.

- Less frequent interaction with family members may lead to reduced socialization.

When deciding between indoor and outdoor housing, consider your ability to meet the rabbit's needs in either setting. Many owners opt for a combination, providing outdoor playtime during favorable weather while housing their rabbits indoors at night or during extreme conditions.

Cage and Hutch Setup: Size, Bedding, and Accessories

The layout and design of your rabbit's enclosure significantly impact its quality of life. A well-equipped habitat should offer enough space, comfortable bedding, and enriching accessories to keep your rabbit healthy and content.

1. **Size**:

Rabbits need sufficient space to move, stretch, and hop around freely. The enclosure should be at least four times the size of your rabbit when fully stretched out, though larger is always better. For larger breeds, such as Flemish Giants or Giant Angoras, even more space is necessary.

- Indoor cages should measure at least 4 x 2 x 2 feet for small breeds, with additional free-roaming time daily.
- Outdoor hutches should include a secure run area, allowing rabbits to exercise and explore.

2. **Bedding**:

Bedding provides insulation, comfort, and a place for rabbits to rest. Choose materials that are safe, absorbent, and easy to clean.

- Recommended Bedding Options:

- Paper-based bedding, such as recycled paper pellets or shredded paper, is soft and dust-free.

- Aspen shavings are a safe wood-based option, unlike pine or cedar shavings, which contain harmful oils.

- Straw can be used for insulation in outdoor setups, especially during colder months.

Avoid:

- Clumping cat litter, as it can be ingested and cause blockages.

- Scented bedding or materials with added chemicals.

3. **Accessories**:

Equip the enclosure with essential accessories to support your rabbit's needs.

- A water bottle or heavy ceramic dish for fresh water.

- A sturdy food dish for pellets and a hay rack for constant access to fresh hay.

- A litter box filled with rabbit-safe litter for easier cleanup and training.

- Hideouts or shelters where the rabbit can retreat for privacy or rest.

- Toys for mental stimulation, such as chew sticks, cardboard tubes, and activity balls.

Ensuring Comfort and Safety in the Environment

A rabbit's environment plays a crucial role in its overall well-being. Whether indoors or outdoors, it's important to prioritize comfort, security, and enrichment.

- **Temperature Control:**

Rabbits are sensitive to temperature extremes and thrive in environments between 60°F and 70°F (15°C–21°C).

For Indoor Housing:

✓ Avoid placing the enclosure near heating vents, air conditioners, or direct sunlight.

✓ Use fans or cooling mats during hot weather to keep the environment comfortable.

For Outdoor Housing:

✓ Provide insulated shelters during winter and shaded areas during summer.

✓ Use weatherproof covers to protect against rain and wind.

- **Security**:

  Rabbits are prey animals and require secure housing to protect them from potential threats.

  ✓ Outdoor enclosures should be predator-proof, with sturdy wire mesh and locks to prevent access by foxes, raccoons, or other animals.

✓ Indoor environments should be rabbit-proofed to remove hazards such as electrical cords, toxic plants, and small objects that could be swallowed.

- **Hygiene and Maintenance**:

Keeping the enclosure clean is vital for preventing disease and maintaining comfort.

✓ Clean litter boxes daily and replace bedding regularly to minimize odors and bacteria buildup.

✓ Disinfect food and water containers weekly.

✓ For outdoor setups, ensure the run and hutch remain free of mud, debris, and standing water.

- **Enrichment and Interaction**:

Rabbits are intelligent and curious animals that need mental stimulation to prevent boredom.

- ✓ Rotate toys and accessories regularly to keep their environment engaging.
- ✓ Provide supervised playtime in a larger area or garden, ensuring it's free of hazards.
- ✓ Spend time interacting with your rabbit through grooming, training, or gentle handling.

Creating the ideal habitat for your rabbit involves careful planning and attention to detail. Whether you choose indoor or outdoor housing, the enclosure must be spacious, secure, and equipped with all the essentials for a comfortable life. By prioritizing their comfort, safety, and enrichment, you can create an environment where your rabbit will not only survive but thrive. Through proper care and consideration, your rabbit's home will become a sanctuary that supports their health, happiness, and unique personality.

CHAPTER FIVE
FEEDING AND NUTRITION

Angora rabbits are beautiful, wool-producing animals known for their thick, luxurious fur and gentle nature. Proper feeding and nutrition play a crucial role in maintaining their health, ensuring optimal wool production, and preventing common health issues. A well-balanced diet tailored to their specific needs not only supports their digestive health but also promotes a shiny, healthy coat. Below, we explore the essential dietary needs of Angora rabbits, suitable treats, and the importance of avoiding harmful foods and overfeeding.

Essential Dietary Needs: Hay, Pellets, and Fresh Greens

The foundation of an Angora rabbit's diet is high-quality hay, which should make up about 80% of their daily food intake. Hay is essential for their digestive system, as it provides the fiber needed to maintain a healthy gut and prevent conditions like gastrointestinal stasis (GI stasis), a common and potentially fatal issue in rabbits. Timothy hay is an excellent choice for adult Angora rabbits, while alfalfa hay, which is higher in calcium and protein, is better suited for growing kits and nursing does. Providing fresh hay daily ensures that your rabbit has constant access to this vital resource.

Pellets serve as a supplemental part of their diet, providing concentrated nutrients such as vitamins, minerals, and protein necessary for wool production. Choose high-quality rabbit pellets specifically formulated without added sugars, fillers, or artificial ingredients. Angora rabbits, because of their wool production, may require pellets with a slightly higher protein content than other rabbit breeds—around 16–18%. However, pellets should be offered in moderation, typically about ¼ cup per 5 pounds of body weight per day, to prevent weight gain and associated health problems.

Fresh greens add variety and essential nutrients to the Angora rabbit's diet. Leafy greens such as romaine lettuce, cilantro, parsley, kale (in moderation), and dandelion greens are excellent choices. Greens not only provide hydration due to their high water content but also contribute to a balanced diet rich in vitamins. Introduce new greens gradually to monitor for any adverse reactions, as sudden changes in diet can upset their sensitive digestive systems.

Safe Fruits and Vegetables as Treats

While hay, pellets, and greens make up the primary diet, fruits and vegetables can be offered occasionally as treats to add enrichment and variety. Safe fruits for Angora rabbits include apples (without seeds), bananas, strawberries, blueberries, and melons. These should be given in small amounts—no more than 1–2 tablespoons per day—as fruits are high in natural sugars that can lead to obesity and digestive issues if consumed in excess.

Vegetables like carrots, bell peppers, zucchini, and cucumber are also suitable as treats. Unlike leafy greens, these vegetables should be provided sparingly to avoid disrupting the rabbit's primary source of nutrition. Offering these foods occasionally can make feeding time more enjoyable for your rabbit, providing mental stimulation and encouraging natural foraging behaviors.

When feeding treats, it's crucial to remember moderation. Overindulging your Angora rabbit in sugary fruits or starchy vegetables can result in weight gain and an imbalance in gut flora. A helpful approach is to think of treats as a small bonus rather than a staple of their diet.

Avoiding Harmful Foods and Overfeeding

Angora rabbits have delicate digestive systems, and certain foods can be harmful or even toxic to them. Foods to strictly avoid include chocolate, avocado, onions, garlic, potatoes, rhubarb, and iceberg lettuce. These foods can cause severe health problems, including gastrointestinal distress, organ failure, or toxicity. Processed human foods, sugary snacks, and dairy products should also never be given to rabbits, as they lack the ability to digest them properly.

Overfeeding, even with healthy foods like pellets or vegetables, can lead to obesity and associated health issues such as joint problems, reduced mobility, and a shorter lifespan. Excessive pellet consumption, for example, can contribute to a lack of appetite for hay, which is vital for maintaining a healthy gut. Similarly, overfeeding vegetables high in oxalates, such as spinach or beet greens, can lead to kidney problems if consumed in large amounts over time.

Another critical aspect of avoiding overfeeding is monitoring portion sizes and establishing a consistent feeding schedule. Provide fresh food at the same time each day, and remove uneaten greens or treats after a few hours to prevent spoilage. Regularly weigh your Angora rabbit and consult a veterinarian if you notice significant weight changes or changes in appetite.

Hydration is another crucial component of a rabbit's diet. Always ensure your Angora rabbit has access to clean, fresh water. A water bottle or heavy ceramic bowl works well to prevent spillage. Rabbits with longer fur, like Angoras, may accidentally dip their fur into their water bowl, so regular cleaning of the bowl and surrounding area is essential.

In summary, Feeding an Angora rabbit requires careful attention to its unique dietary needs, balancing hay, pellets, and fresh greens while incorporating occasional treats for variety. Avoiding harmful foods and monitoring portion sizes are equally important to maintain their health and well-being. By providing a thoughtful, well-rounded diet, you ensure that your Angora rabbit thrives, producing luxurious wool and enjoying a long, healthy life as a cherished companion.

CHAPTER SIX
GROOMING AND WOOL MANAGEMENT

Angora rabbits are prized for their luxurious, soft wool, but maintaining the quality of their coat requires diligent grooming and wool management practices. Regular grooming not only enhances the appearance of the rabbit but also prevents potential health issues associated with their dense fur. Here, we will explore daily and weekly grooming practices, methods for preventing and managing matting, and proper techniques for harvesting and caring for Angora wool.

Daily and Weekly Grooming Practices

1. **Daily Maintenance**: Daily grooming is essential for Angora rabbits, especially during the molting season. Use a slicker brush or a wide-tooth

comb to remove loose fibers and detangle small knots. This prevents the wool from accumulating and creating mats, which can lead to discomfort or skin irritation. Daily checks also help in spotting any debris or parasites, such as mites, that might hide in the dense wool.

2. Weekly Deep Grooming: A more thorough grooming session should be conducted once a week. This involves using a combination of grooming tools, such as undercoat rakes and fine-toothed combs, to ensure the coat is free of tangles and mats. Pay extra attention to areas prone to matting, such as behind the ears, under the armpits, and around the tail. These sessions are also an opportunity to check for signs of skin issues, wounds, or infections that might be hidden under the thick fur.

3. Clipping and Trimming: For Angoras with exceptionally long coats, periodic trimming may be necessary. Clipping the wool around sensitive areas, such as the face, paws, and genital area, helps maintain hygiene and reduces the risk of soiling and infections. Electric clippers or sharp scissors can be used carefully to avoid accidental cuts.

Preventing and Managing Matting

1. Understanding Mat Formation: Matting occurs when the wool fibers tangle and clump together, creating dense, tight patches that are difficult to untangle. Mats often form in high-friction areas or where grooming is insufficient. Factors such as moisture, dirt, and infrequent grooming exacerbate the problem.

2. Preventive Measures: Regular grooming is the most effective way to prevent matting. Ensure that the rabbit's environment is clean and dry, as dampness encourages mat formation. Providing the rabbit with clean bedding and minimizing exposure to elements that could dirty the coat, such as damp grass or hay, can also help.

3. Dealing with Mats: When mats do form, they must be addressed promptly to avoid discomfort or skin irritation. Small mats can be gently teased apart using a comb or mat splitter. For larger or more stubborn mats, carefully cutting them out with scissors is often the safest approach. Always hold the mat away from the skin to avoid accidental cuts. For severe matting that covers large areas, seeking assistance from a professional groomer or veterinarian may be necessary.

Harvesting and Caring for Angora Wool

1. **Harvesting Techniques**: Angora wool can be harvested through shearing, plucking, or brushing, depending on the rabbit's breed and the growth phase of the wool. Shearing

involves using electric clippers or scissors to cut the wool close to the skin, typically every three months. Plucking is a gentler method suited for breeds that naturally molt; loose fibers are gently pulled out by hand during molting seasons. Brushing, though less common, is effective for collecting loose wool during regular grooming sessions.

2. **Handling the Wool**: After harvesting, it is crucial to clean and sort the wool. Remove any debris, such as hay or straw, and separate the fibers based on their length and quality. Longer fibers are ideal for spinning, while shorter fibers may be used for felting. Washing the wool in warm, soapy water removes natural oils and dirt. Ensure the wool is thoroughly rinsed and dried to prevent mildew or odors.

3. **Storage and Maintenance**: Store Angora wool in a dry, cool environment to preserve its quality. Use breathable containers, such as

cotton bags, to protect the fibers from dust and pests. Adding cedar chips or lavender sachets to the storage area can help deter moths and other insects that might damage the wool. Periodically check stored wool to ensure it remains clean and free of infestations.

By adhering to a consistent grooming and wool management routine, Angora rabbit owners can maintain their pets' health and comfort while ensuring a steady supply of high-quality wool. Grooming not only enhances the rabbit's overall well-being but also solidifies the bond between the owner and their furry companion.

CHAPTER SEVEN
HEALTH AND WELLNESS

Angora rabbits, known for their luxurious, long coats, are a distinct and delightful breed requiring special attention to their health and wellness. Like all pets, they are susceptible to a range of health issues that require keen observation, proper care, and preventive measures to ensure they live long, healthy lives. Angora rabbits, due to their unique grooming needs and active metabolism, are particularly prone to certain health concerns, including gastrointestinal (GI) stasis, parasites, and wool block. By understanding these common health issues, recognizing the signs of illness or stress, and providing proactive care, owners can significantly enhance the quality of life for their Angora rabbits.

Common Health Issues: GI Stasis, Parasites, and Wool Block

Angora rabbits, like all rabbits, have specific health risks related to their digestive system, skin, and overall well-being. Being aware of these issues is key to effective management and care.

1. GI Stasis

Gastrointestinal stasis, or GI stasis, is a common and potentially life-threatening condition in rabbits. It occurs when the digestive system slows down or stops entirely, preventing food from moving through the intestines. This can lead to severe discomfort, bloating, and even death if not treated promptly.

- **Causes:** GI stasis can be caused by stress, inadequate diet (especially a lack of fiber), dehydration, or a sudden change in the environment. Angora rabbits, due to their high-fiber diet requirements, can be particularly vulnerable to GI issues.

- **Symptoms:** Common symptoms include loss of appetite, lethargy, smaller, fewer droppings, bloating, and abdominal pain. If left untreated, the condition can become fatal.

- **Treatment:** Immediate veterinary care is required for rabbits suffering from GI stasis. Treatment often involves fluid therapy, gentle massage, and medication to stimulate the digestive tract. In severe cases, surgery may be necessary.

2. Parasites

Rabbits, including Angoras, can also be affected by various external and internal parasites. Common parasites include fleas, mites, and intestinal worms, which can cause severe discomfort, hair loss, skin irritation, and digestive issues.

- **External Parasites:** Fleas and mites can infest Angora rabbits, especially if they are kept outdoors or in unclean environments. Symptoms include itching, hair loss, scabs, and red or inflamed skin. Regular grooming and cleaning of the rabbit's environment are essential for parasite prevention.

- **Internal Parasites:** Worms and other intestinal parasites can disrupt digestion and cause symptoms like diarrhea, weight loss, and lethargy. Regular fecal tests by a veterinarian are essential to detect and treat internal parasites.

3. Wool Block

Wool block, or hairballs, is a significant health issue for Angora rabbits due to their long, dense coats. These rabbits shed large amounts of fur, which they can inadvertently ingest while grooming themselves. The ingested fur can cause blockages in the digestive system, leading to wool block.

- **Causes:** The primary cause of wool block is excessive fur ingestion, which can build up in the rabbit's stomach or intestines, leading to discomfort, pain, and potentially dangerous blockages.

- **Symptoms:** Common signs of wool block include loss of appetite, lethargy, bloating, and difficulty passing stool. In severe cases, it can lead to GI stasis.

- **Treatment and Prevention:** Regular grooming is critical to preventing wool block. Brushing the Angora rabbit daily helps to remove loose fur before it can be ingested. Additionally, offering a high-fiber diet (such as hay) helps with digestion, and providing digestive supplements, like papaya or pineapple enzymes, can help break down hairballs. In severe cases, a veterinarian may need to manually remove the blockage or administer medications.

Recognizing Signs of Illness or Stress

Recognizing early signs of illness or stress in Angora rabbits is crucial for preventing more serious health issues. Rabbits are prey animals and often hide symptoms of illness until it becomes severe. Therefore, vigilance and regular observation are key to catching problems early.

1. Signs of Illness

- **Loss of Appetite:** A sudden lack of interest in food is often one of the first signs that something is wrong. It can indicate GI stasis, dental issues, or other health problems. If a rabbit refuses to eat hay, fresh vegetables, or pellets for more than 12 hours, it is a cause for concern.

- **Changes in Behavior:** Rabbits that are normally active may become lethargic, withdrawn, or exhibit signs of pain, such as hunched posture or grinding their teeth. Painful conditions like GI stasis or injury can cause this behavior.

- **Respiratory Issues:** Labored breathing, nasal discharge, or excessive sneezing can indicate respiratory infections. Rabbits are susceptible to conditions like snuffles, which require immediate veterinary attention.

- **Changes in Droppings:** Healthy rabbits produce small, round, firm droppings. A decrease in the quantity or size of droppings, or the presence of diarrhea or soft stools, can be a sign of gastrointestinal distress.

- **Hair Loss and Skin Issues:** Fur loss, skin rashes, or visible sores can be signs of parasitic infections, fungal infections, or even stress. Regular grooming and inspection of the coat can help detect these issues early.

2. Signs of Stress

Stress can severely impact a rabbit's health and immune system. Angora rabbits can be particularly sensitive to stress due to their high grooming needs and temperament. Stress can result from environmental changes, lack of social interaction, or overcrowding.

- **Physical Symptoms of Stress:** Stressed rabbits may exhibit rapid breathing, excessive grooming, or a loss of appetite. They may also show signs of aggression or biting, indicating they feel threatened or overwhelmed.

- **Behavioral Symptoms of Stress:** A rabbit experiencing stress may refuse to interact, hide frequently, or show signs of aggression or hyperactivity. They may also engage in destructive behaviors like chewing on cage bars or digging excessively.

Understanding these signs and promptly addressing the underlying cause can prevent stress from affecting the rabbit's health.

Preventative Care and Veterinary Visits

Regular care and veterinary check-ups are essential for maintaining the health and well-being of your Angora rabbit. Preventive care can help catch potential health issues early and ensure that your rabbit lives a long and comfortable life.

1. Regular Grooming

One of the most crucial aspects of Angora rabbit care is regular grooming. Angoras need daily brushing to prevent matting and reduce the risk of wool block. Regular grooming also allows owners to check for parasites, skin conditions, or any signs of illness.

- **Nail Clipping:** Regular nail clipping is necessary to prevent overgrown nails, which can cause discomfort and mobility issues.

- **Dental Health:** Rabbits' teeth grow continuously, so a diet that promotes dental wear (such as hay and chew toys) is important for preventing dental problems, which can lead to malocclusion and painful abscesses.

2. Regular Veterinary Check-Ups

Routine visits to an experienced rabbit veterinarian are crucial for monitoring your rabbit's overall health. These check-ups can help detect early signs of illness or parasite infestations that may not be immediately apparent.

- **Vaccinations and Parasite Control:** Ensure your Angora rabbit is up to date with any necessary vaccinations and parasite prevention treatments. Rabbits can suffer from diseases like rabbit hemorrhagic disease (RHD), which can be prevented through vaccination.

- **Annual Health Screenings:** A full annual check-up, including a dental examination, is vital to ensure your rabbit's health. These screenings often include blood tests, fecal exams, and physical assessments to check for any hidden issues.

3. Environmental Enrichment

Creating a stress-free, enriching environment is vital for your Angora rabbit's health. Providing ample space to hop, chew, and explore ensures that your rabbit remains physically and mentally stimulated. Safe, interactive toys, chewing options, and a clean living area can help reduce stress and promote well-being.

In conclusion, maintaining the health and wellness of an Angora rabbit involves a combination of preventative care, regular health monitoring, and addressing specific breed-related issues such as GI stasis, parasites, and wool block. By recognizing the signs of illness or stress early and providing proactive care, owners can ensure their rabbits remain happy, healthy, and well-adjusted. With regular grooming, veterinary visits, and a properly enriched environment, your Angora rabbit can thrive and lead a fulfilling life.

CHAPTER EIGHT
BREEDING AND RAISING ANGORA RABBITS

Breeding and raising Angora rabbits can be a rewarding but challenging experience. This process requires careful planning, attention to detail, and a strong understanding of rabbit biology, behavior, and welfare. Angora rabbits, with their unique long coats, need specialized care throughout their breeding and rearing stages. Whether you're considering breeding Angoras for their wool, companionship, or for expanding a rabbitry, it's essential to ensure the health and well-being of both the parents and their offspring. This comprehensive guide will provide insights into mating and nesting behavior, caring for kits, and socializing young rabbits.

Mating and Nesting Behavior

Mating Behavior in Angora Rabbits

When breeding Angora rabbits, it's important to first ensure that both the doe (female) and buck (male) are in good health. Only rabbits that are free from diseases, parasites, and genetic issues should be bred. Additionally, both rabbits should be mature enough, typically around 6 months of age for smaller Angora breeds, although larger breeds may take a little longer to reach sexual maturity.

- **Courtship Rituals:** Mating behavior in Angora rabbits typically begins with a courtship ritual. The doe will signal her readiness to mate by becoming more receptive to the male's advances. This may involve the doe sniffing, licking, or nuzzling the male. The male will often circle the doe and may even perform a "buck dance," a behavior in which he will nudge or lightly nudge her with his nose.

- **Mating Process:** When the doe is ready, she will allow the buck to mount. After mating, the doe may become more territorial and may display some protective behavior over her space. The actual mating process is brief, lasting only a few minutes. Following successful mating, the doe will typically go into a period of rest and will start nesting behaviors shortly afterward.

Nesting Behavior

After mating, the doe will begin preparing for the birth of her kits. This process is instinctive and is driven by hormonal changes in her body. Angora rabbits, like other rabbits, are known for building nests using materials available in their environment. However, it's essential to provide proper nesting materials to encourage safe and comfortable birth conditions.

- **Creating a Nesting Box:** A nesting box should be placed in the doe's enclosure a few days before the expected due date. The box should be spacious, made of a non-toxic material, and filled with soft bedding such as straw or hay. The bedding should be deep enough to allow the doe to burrow, but not so deep that it poses a risk of suffocating the kits. Avoid using materials like cedar shavings, which can be harmful to rabbits.

- **Preparing the Nest:** As the birth date approaches, the doe will instinctively begin to pull out some of her fur, creating a soft and warm bedding for her kits. This fur acts as insulation to keep the kits warm in the early stages of their life. It's important not to disturb the doe during this process, as it's a natural and necessary part of the nesting behavior.

- **Birth of Kits:** The actual birth process, known as kindling, can take place within a few hours. Typically, the doe will give birth to a litter of between 4 to 8 kits, though this number can vary. The kits are born blind, hairless, and completely dependent on their mother for warmth, food, and care.

Caring for Kits: From Birth to Weaning

Once the kits are born, the primary responsibility shifts to the doe, but the breeder should still be vigilant in ensuring the health and safety of both the doe and her young. **Rabbit kits** are born blind, deaf, and hairless, making them entirely dependent on their mother for warmth and nourishment. The doe will nurse her kits by providing her milk, which is rich in nutrients essential for the kits' growth and development. It is important to ensure that the doe is well-fed during this time to ensure she has enough milk for her kits. Providing a nutritious diet that includes hay, fresh greens, and a balanced pellet mix is crucial for her health and milk production.

The kits should remain in the nest, with the doe only coming out for short intervals to eat or drink. The doe will typically nurse the kits only once or twice a day, usually during the night, so it may be difficult for the breeder to observe directly. However, if the kits are growing well and appear healthy, with a steady increase in size, it's usually a sign that the doe is feeding them adequately.

As the kits grow, they will begin to develop fur, open their eyes, and start to explore the nest. By the age of **3 to 4 weeks**, kits will begin nibbling on solid food, primarily hay, which they will continue to eat alongside their mother's milk. The process of weaning usually occurs at around **6 to 8 weeks**. During this time, the kits should be offered a variety of high-fiber foods, such as hay and fresh vegetables, to encourage the transition to solid food.

It's important to closely monitor the health of the kits during their early stages. Any kits that appear lethargic, underweight, or fail to thrive should be given immediate attention. In some cases, hand-feeding may be necessary, though this should only be done under the guidance of a veterinarian or an experienced breeder. Kits should be kept in a clean, safe, and stress-free environment to ensure they continue to grow strong and healthy. The breeder should also monitor the doe's condition after birth to ensure she is recovering well and not showing signs of illness or fatigue, such as loss of appetite or reluctance to care for the kits.

Socializing Young Rabbits

Socializing Angora rabbit kits is an essential step in their development. Early socialization helps ensure that the young rabbits grow up to be friendly, calm, and easy to handle, which makes them better pets or potential show animals. When kits are born, they are naturally fearful of new environments and unfamiliar handling, but they will gradually become accustomed to their caretakers as they age.

At around **3 to 4 weeks**, the kits begin to explore their environment and will start responding to human interaction. It's important to handle the kits gently during this period to ensure they become accustomed to human contact. Picking up the kits regularly in a calm and gentle manner will help them feel more comfortable being held. However, it's important not to over-handle them, as excessive stress can cause behavioral issues in the future. Each kit should be treated with care, and breeders should be patient, allowing the kits to develop trust at their own pace.

Once the kits are weaned at around **6 to 8 weeks**, they should be gradually introduced to other rabbits or pets in the household, depending on the breeder's plans for the kits. Introducing them to other rabbits should be done slowly and in a controlled manner to prevent territorial aggression. If the goal is to socialize the kits as family pets, it's essential to continue positive reinforcement training and handling.

By **12 weeks of age**, the kits should be well-socialized and accustomed to regular handling, grooming, and human interaction. Early socialization is vital not only for emotional and behavioral development but also to ensure the kits become adaptable and confident in their new homes. If they are intended for sale or adoption, proper socialization ensures that they will thrive in their new environments and build strong, lasting bonds with their future owners.

Overall, breeding and raising Angora rabbits requires a significant amount of commitment and care, but by following best practices in mating, nest preparation, caring for the kits, and socialization, breeders can ensure that both the doe and the kits thrive. This process is essential for ensuring the health, well-being, and future success of the rabbits, whether they are being raised for their wool, as pets, or for other purposes.

CHAPTER NINE
LONG-TERM CARE AND LIFESTYLE

Angora rabbits are unique and charming creatures, known for their soft, luxurious coats and gentle temperament. However, owning an Angora rabbit requires a thorough understanding of their long-term care needs, as they require more maintenance than other rabbit breeds due to their dense fur and specific lifestyle demands. From lifespan and age-specific care to social interaction and enrichment activities, there are several key factors to consider to ensure your Angora rabbit lives a happy and healthy life.

Lifespan and Age-Specific Needs

Angora rabbits typically have a lifespan of 7 to 12 years, although with proper care, some can live even longer. This relatively long lifespan means that their care needs change as they grow from a playful young rabbit to an older, more sedentary companion. It's important to tailor your care approach based on the rabbit's age to ensure that it remains healthy and comfortable throughout its life.

1. Young Angora Rabbits (0-1 year): When Angora rabbits are young, they are incredibly active and curious. During this time, they require a balanced diet rich in hay, fresh vegetables, and limited pellets. This is also the stage where they need socialization and early training to adapt to life as a pet. Their coats are growing in during this time, and they are especially prone to mats and tangles, so regular grooming is crucial. Young rabbits also need plenty of space to hop, explore, and exercise to develop their muscles and avoid obesity.

2. Adult Angora Rabbits (1-7 years): As Angora rabbits mature, their exercise needs remain high, but their overall activity level may begin to decrease somewhat as they become more accustomed to their environment. This period requires careful attention to diet to prevent obesity, a common issue for indoor rabbits. Regular grooming becomes even more essential during this phase as their coats reach full density, and matting can occur if left untreated. Adult rabbits are also more likely to develop health conditions like dental problems, so routine veterinary checkups are crucial.

3. Senior Angora Rabbits (7 years and older): Older Angora rabbits typically experience a decrease in energy levels and may be less active. It's important to make adjustments to their environment to accommodate potential mobility issues. Providing softer bedding and easy access to food and water is essential. Additionally, senior rabbits are at higher risk for health issues such as arthritis, dental disease, and digestive problems, so regular veterinary visits are necessary. Their coats may also require more intensive grooming as their ability to groom themselves decreases. Special care should be taken to monitor their weight and appetite, as loss of appetite can be a sign of underlying health problems.

Social Interaction and Enrichment Activities

Angora rabbits are highly social animals that thrive on companionship and mental stimulation. They are naturally curious and enjoy exploring their environment, which makes enrichment activities a vital part of their long-term care.

Socialization:

One of the most important aspects of keeping an Angora rabbit is providing adequate social interaction. Rabbits are herd animals in the wild, and while domesticated rabbits can live alone, they require regular human interaction to stay emotionally healthy. Ideally, they should not be left alone for long periods of time, as loneliness can lead to depression and behavioral issues such as chewing or destructive behavior. If you are unable to spend a lot of time with your rabbit, consider adopting another rabbit as a companion. Just make sure to properly introduce them to avoid territorial disputes.

Enrichment Activities:

To keep an Angora rabbit mentally and physically stimulated, provide a variety of enrichment activities. This can include toys such as wooden chew blocks, tunnels, and cardboard boxes. These not only help wear down their teeth (which constantly grow) but also keep their minds active. Rabbits also enjoy foraging, so hide treats around their enclosure or home to encourage natural hunting behaviors.

Daily playtime outside their cage or enclosure is also essential for their well-being. Angora rabbits love hopping and exploring new spaces, so create a safe, enclosed area for them to exercise in. In addition, regular grooming sessions serve as both a bonding activity and a form of enrichment.

Tips for Ensuring a Happy and Healthy Rabbit

Ensuring the health and happiness of your Angora rabbit requires a combination of proper care, attention to their needs, and commitment to their well-being. Here are several tips to make sure you provide the best environment and lifestyle for your furry companion:

1. Regular Grooming:

Angora rabbits are famous for their thick, woolly fur, which grows continuously. Without regular grooming, their coats can become matted and tangled, causing discomfort or even leading to serious health issues like skin infections or restricted blood flow. Grooming should be done daily to keep their coats tangle-free and prevent matting. A fine-toothed comb or slicker brush works well for this purpose. Keep an eye on the undercoat, as it can get tangled easily and lead to painful mats. During molting periods, when they shed large amounts of fur, grooming is especially critical to avoid overgrowth and fur blockages.

2. A Healthy, Balanced Diet:

As with all rabbits, a healthy diet is critical. For Angora rabbits, hay should be the foundation of their diet, supplemented by fresh vegetables, fruits, and limited pellets. Ensure they have unlimited access to fresh hay, which provides essential fiber for digestion and prevents obesity. Fresh greens such as parsley, cilantro, and dandelion leaves should be offered daily. Occasional fruits like apples (without seeds) or berries can be given as treats, but they should be limited due to their high sugar content. Fresh water should always be available, either in a water bottle or a heavy bowl to prevent spills.

3. A Spacious, Safe Environment:

Angora rabbits require plenty of space to hop around and exercise. A rabbit hutch or pen should be large enough to allow for movement and to prevent boredom. If they live indoors, consider giving them access to a larger room or an outdoor playpen where they can stretch their legs. They also need a quiet, safe place to sleep, away from high-traffic areas. Provide soft bedding such as hay or shredded paper, avoiding cedar or pine shavings, which can be harmful to their respiratory health.

4. Regular Veterinary Checkups:

Routine veterinary visits are an important part of ensuring your Angora rabbit remains healthy. Your rabbit should be checked at least once a year, but older rabbits or those with health issues may require more frequent visits. The vet will examine their teeth, eyes, and digestive health, as well as check for signs of common rabbit ailments such as respiratory infections, parasites, or dental disease. Ensure your rabbit is up-to-date on vaccinations and is spayed or neutered if necessary.

5. Mental and Physical Exercise:

Angora rabbits need both mental and physical stimulation to thrive. In addition to their regular social interaction, provide activities that engage their natural curiosity. Set up obstacle courses with tunnels, boxes, and toys to encourage physical movement. Rotate toys and challenges regularly to keep things interesting.

CONCLUSION

In conclusion, owning an Angora rabbit is a rewarding experience that requires dedication, patience, and a deep understanding of their unique needs. From their meticulous grooming requirements to their need for social interaction and mental stimulation, these fluffy companions thrive in an environment that provides both physical and emotional care. By offering a balanced diet, regular veterinary care, and a safe, enriching environment, you can ensure that your Angora rabbit leads a healthy, happy, and long life. Whether you are a first-time rabbit owner or a seasoned enthusiast, the bond you share with your Angora rabbit will undoubtedly be filled with joy and fulfillment, making the effort you put into their care well worth it.

THANKS FOR READING.